COLD WAR SPY STORIES

BY EMMA HUDDLESTON

MOMENTUM

The Child's World®
childsworld.com

Published by The Child's World®
1980 Lookout Drive • Mankato, MN 56003-1705
800-599-READ • www.childsworld.com

Photographs ©: Shutterstock Images, cover
(camera), cover (rockets), 1 (camera), 1 (rockets);
FW Studio/Shutterstock Images, cover
(background), 1 (background); AVS-Images/
Shutterstock Images, cover (photo frame), 1 (photo
frame); Everett Historical/Shutterstock Images, 5,
12; Everett Collection Inc/Alamy, 6; AP Images, 8,
9, 28; Sovfoto Universal Images Group/Newscom,
10; Red Line Editorial, 13; Bob Daugherty/AP
Images, 14; Ron Edmonds/AP Images, 16; Donald
Traill/AP Images, 18, 23; Dennis Brack/Black Star/
Newscom, 20; Aston's/Splash/ SplashNews/
Newscom, 21; Lisa Blue/iStockphoto, 24; Pavel L
Photo and Video/Shutterstock Images, 26

ISBN 9781503844834 (Reinforced Library Binding)
ISBN 9781503847279 (Portable Document Format)
ISBN 9781503848467 (Online Multi-user eBook
LCCN 2019956604

Printed in the United States of America

CONTENTS

MOMENTUM

FAST FACTS

What Was the Cold War?

▶ The Cold War began after World War II (1939–1945) ended. It was not an all-out war. The Cold War was, in part, a political conflict between the United States and the **Soviet Union**.

▶ The United States and the Soviet Union battled each other in proxy wars. Proxy wars are wars fought in other countries. During the Cold War, the United States would back one side while the Soviet Union supported the other. The Vietnam War (1954–1975) was a proxy war. The United States backed South Vietnam. The Soviet Union backed North Vietnam and tried to help them take over South Vietnam.

▶ The United States and the Soviet Union, which included Russia, both wanted a strong military with powerful weapons. People feared that the two countries would use powerful **nuclear** weapons against each other.

▶ The Cold War ended in 1991. The Soviet Union broke up into 15 independent nations. One of these nations is Russia.

Spies and Their Tools

▶ Spies gathered **intelligence** about scientific advances and how to make weapons.

▲ The United States sent planes and troops into Vietnam.

► Spy gadgets often combined technology with everyday objects. For example, a transmitter could be hidden in the heel of a shoe. A transmitter was made of a microphone, wires, and a battery. It picked up sounds such as people talking. Nearby receiver radios could listen in.

► The Soviet Union invented a camera hidden in a coat. The camera's tiny lens was in a button. This invention made it easy for spies to take pictures.

► The U.S. Central Intelligence Agency (CIA) invented a tiny flying vehicle that could take photos.

CHAPTER ONE

SOLVING SOVIET CODES

Angeline Nanni sat at a desk. She looked at the rows of complicated numbers on the paper in front of her. She was at Arlington Hall in Virginia. The girls' school had been turned into a secret government building. Nanni tapped a pencil on the hard desk. The paper before her was a test. If she passed, she could get a job. But she didn't yet know what the job would be.

Suddenly, Nanni saw how the numbers added together. She subtracted some numbers and circled others. She wrote down the extra numbers in the set as the answer. The few other women in the room were still working. Nanni showed her paper to the instructor. The instructor smiled wide. Nanni had solved the difficult problem. She was going to become part of a small Soviet code-breaking team for the U.S. government. The team was going to figure out secrets in Soviet messages.

◄ **The U.S. government believed that a Soviet attack was a big threat. The government built some underground shelters to protect people.**

▲ In the mid-1950s, the CIA had spy equipment in an underground tunnel in Berlin, Germany. This helped them listen to Russian phone calls. At the time, Russia controlled part of Berlin.

Nanni joined the Venona team in 1945. Most people on the team were women. Only the Venona women really knew that their work was to break Soviet codes. Each day, Nanni walked to a small back room. It was the office space for Venona, and only her team was allowed inside. At the end of each day, Nanni helped pack up the office for extra security. She rolled up maps. She locked all papers inside cabinets.

At times, solving a Soviet code seemed impossible. The Soviets were known for making unbreakable codes. And they often used a code only once. However, a computer helped Nanni sort through thousands of Soviet messages. It used paper cards with holes punched into them according to a code.

▲ **The Venona team helped uncover Soviet spies such as Ethel and Julius Rosenberg.**

A punched card helped the computer read a message that was written from that code. Nanni pushed messages through the computer and changed out the punch cards. Eventually, the computer showed that some one-time codes had been used twice! Nanni and the team could compare messages made from the same codes.

The Venona women looked over old messages to see if they could make sense of them. They uncovered the names of Soviet spies. They even found evidence that the government could use to bring the spies to justice.

CHAPTER TWO

STOPPING THE CUBAN MISSILE CRISIS

O leg Penkovsky strode into a building with a telephone in the entrance area. He was in the Soviet Union. In Penkovsky's pocket was a small matchbox. Inside, he hid a tiny disc that stored photos of secret information. The matchbox was wrapped with a soft green wire. The end of the wire was bent into a hook shape. Penkovsky used the telephone, but it wasn't the reason he went to that location. He looked around. Then, he hung the matchbox on a hook behind a green radiator in the room. A CIA agent would pick up the information later.

Penkovsky was a colonel in the Soviet military intelligence unit. He was the highest-level officer to spy for the United States during the Cold War. The reason he wanted to spy was because he disagreed with Soviet Union leader Nikita Khrushchev's goal of spreading **communism** throughout world.

◄ Oleg Penkovsky (right) risked his freedom to spy for the United States.

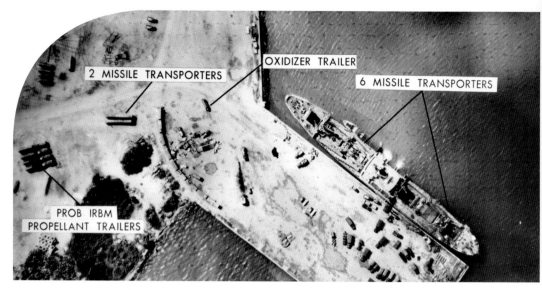

▲ U.S. forces snapped secret photos of Soviet missiles in Cuba.

During 1961 and 1962, Penkovsky traveled to Great Britain and France three times. He was a Soviet leader for scientific research. He arranged secret meetings with British and U.S. agents on his trips. He spoke with them for hours. He delivered rolls of film and photos. He gave detailed descriptions of Soviet plans for **missile** launch sites in Cuba. His knowledge was very valuable.

Penkovsky's knowledge was especially important in 1962, when the Soviets planted missiles in Cuba. The missiles could carry and direct nuclear weapons across long distances. The Soviet Union could attack the United States with them from Cuba. The two countries were on the brink of war. That situation was known as the Cuban missile crisis.

With Penkovsky's spy work, the United States could track Soviet missile sites. It used technology to measure the readiness of Soviet weapons. Penkovsky's information revealed that the Soviet Union was less prepared than it said it was. Knowing the Soviets were unprepared gave the United States an advantage. President John F. Kennedy knew he had time to **negotiate**. War did not break out because the two countries eventually reached an agreement. The Soviet Union removed its missiles from Cuba.

NUMBER OF NUCLEAR WEAPONS

Experts estimated how many nuclear weapons the United States and Soviet Union/Russia had between 1945 and 2019.

— U.S. Weapons

---- Soviet/ Russian Weapons

Nuclear Weapons

Year

CHAPTER THREE

TRADING SECRETS FOR CASH

John Walker Jr. drove his car from Norfolk, Virginia, to Washington, DC, in 1967. A few secret papers were folded in his pocket. The papers were copies of documents from his work. Walker worked at a U.S. naval base. But he wasn't delivering the papers for his job. He had snuck them out of the base. He was taking them to the Soviet **embassy** in Washington, DC. He wanted to trade U.S. naval secrets for cash as a spy.

Walker pulled into the embassy parking lot. He was nervous, but he focused on his plan. Walker took a deep breath and grabbed the papers. He walked in the front doors of the large stone building. Once inside, he asked to see a security officer. He spoke to a couple people. Walker said he wanted to spy on the United States. Then, he offered the papers as a sample of secrets he could give.

◄ **John Walker Jr. (left) was in the navy for 20 years.**

▲ **Walker encouraged his brother, son, and a friend to spy on the U.S. government, too.**

The Soviets accepted his offer. Walker became one of the Soviet Union's spies.

For more than ten years, Walker spied for the Soviet Union. He gave up U.S. codes, which let the Soviets decode U.S. messages easily. Walker also gave them secret naval communications. Information he passed on helped the Soviets track the movements of U.S. ships.

Sometimes, Walker snuck papers into his office and out of the building. Other times he took pictures with a microdot camera. Microdot cameras shrank the image of a full page of paper. The tiny photographs could be hidden in rings, letters, and coins. Then, Walker scheduled times to drop off information at random locations.

Eventually, his wife, Barbara, found a grocery bag full of secret documents. She held the bag in front of Walker and demanded to know what was going on. He decided to tell Barbara that he was spying. She did nothing at first, but in 1984 she tipped off the FBI. When Walker drove to Maryland to drop off information in 1985, he didn't know the FBI was following him. He left a package for the Soviets with 127 papers in it. The FBI arrested him. He was sentenced to spend the rest of his life in jail.

CAUGHT BY A COIN

Rudolf Abel was a spy for the Soviets. He used hollow coins to hide microdot images and pass it on. Once, he paid a newspaper boy with a hollow coin. The boy reported the fake money. That led to Abel being caught.

CHAPTER FOUR

DEAD DROPS

In 1975, Martha Peterson zoomed down the streets of Moscow, Russia, in a new car. She stopped at a grocery store. Then, she parked her car in a random lot for several minutes. Peterson was on her first CIA mission. She had to find out whether she was being followed.

While she drove, she listened to the tiny earbuds in her ears. They were connected to a radio she wore under her shirt. The radio was tuned to one station. It would pick up Soviet spy radio signals. If the Soviets were following her, she would hear them talking about her movements. But for months, Peterson heard nothing on her drives.

Peterson joined the CIA in 1973. Two years later, she went to Moscow to spy on Soviet officials. She worked at the U.S. embassy in the city. She was the only woman in that CIA station.

◄ **Martha Peterson wrote a book about her time as a spy.**

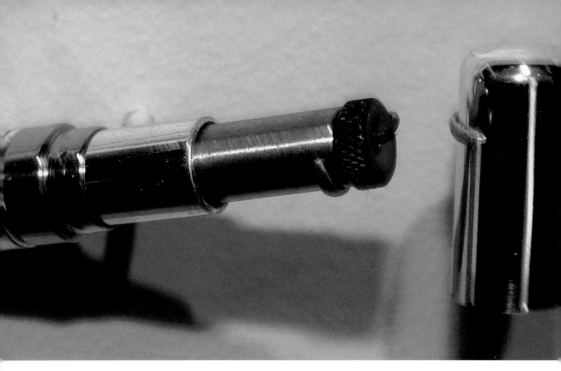

▲ **Some Cold War spies had weapons. One weapon was a lipstick pistol. It was a gun created in the shape of a lipstick container.**

The Soviets underestimated Peterson because she was a woman. They didn't even suspect she was a spy because of her gender. For that reason, Peterson was perfect for dead drops. A dead drop involved agents leaving items for each other at a certain location and never meeting face-to-face. Since Peterson wasn't being followed, she could use the same location multiple times without the Soviets knowing.

Peterson began working with an undercover agent named Trigon. Trigon was a Soviet official. The papers on his desk were highly **classified**. They showed what Soviet leaders were thinking and doing each day.

▲ **Spies hid cameras in things such as purses and jackets.**

The CIA gave Trigon a pen with a microdot camera hidden inside. He took the top off, then clicked the pen to take a picture of the paper on the desk below him. One roll of the tiny film could hold 60 to 80 images. Trigon left the film, along with handwritten notes, in secret spots for Peterson. Then, her team would send the information to Washington, DC.

On the day of a drop, Peterson first drove for 2.5 hours around Moscow. She listened to her radio to see if the Soviets were on to her. If she heard nothing, she would continue. Next, she rode multiple trains. Eventually, Peterson walked from the train station to a park—that's where one of the drop sites was.

Peterson walked on a path under some trees. She passed numbered lampposts. At the right number, she dropped her package. Peterson often used a fake log as the package. The CIA made it in a lab. The center of the log was hollow. The CIA filled it with items for Trigon. They gave him pens, money, cameras and new film, and notes. Trigon often used a crumpled milk carton or an old glove for his own drops for Peterson in that area. These objects wouldn't seem important to anyone who saw them lying on the ground.

Peterson and Trigon were a good team until April 1977. Then, Peterson noticed Trigon's actions changed. One day at the park drop site, a car was parked by the road. She had never seen that before. Also, she saw Trigon hadn't picked up her package from near the lamppost. She and the team were worried that Trigon had been discovered by the Soviets.

In June, Trigon didn't show up for a dead drop. So the U.S. team decided to try and reach him one more time. They scheduled a dead drop for July 15. It was on a bridge over the Moscow River. Peterson's feet clapped softly on the pavement. She walked to a small tower that was part of the bridge. The tower had an opening on both sides that people could walk through.

▲ **Peterson's bag was sometimes used for dead drops.**

Peterson walked in one side of the tower and stopped. She reached into her purse and pulled out a small package. She left it on the ledge of the small window in the stone wall. Quickly, she turned around and walked back out of the tower. She went down the stairs of the bridge, and at the bottom a group of Soviet men grabbed her arms. Then, another Soviet ran down the stairs holding the package that Peterson had just put in the tower window. She had been caught. The Soviets arrested her, but since she worked for the U.S. embassy, she was let go the next day. Trigon wasn't so lucky. The team found out that he died at least one month before Peterson's capture and release.

CHAPTER FIVE

NOTES IN CARS

In January 1977, Adolf Tolkachev waited at a gas station in Moscow. He pulled the collar of his coat tighter to his face. The weather was cold. Finally, a car with a U.S. license plate pulled in. Tolkachev walked to the driver. He checked that the man was American. Then, he left a folded note on the man's car seat and walked away. The note said that Tolkachev wanted to speak with a U.S. official about secret matters. Tolkachev was a Soviet electronics **engineer**, and he was trying to become a spy for the United States.

The American man at the gas station was puzzled. He was the CIA chief in the U.S. embassy in Moscow. But the CIA didn't know whether they could trust Tolkachev. For more than a year, Tolkachev contacted the chief. He passed notes pleading to meet in private.

◄ **Moscow is Russia's biggest city.**

▲ **Both the United States and Soviet Union wanted to be the most advanced country. They built nuclear weapons to help make that happen.**

The notes contained some information about Soviet technology. They also suggested places to meet. But the CIA didn't respond. It didn't want to fall into a Soviet trap.

In March 1978, Tolkachev gave a final letter. It included a map showing where to secretly meet. It also included 11 pages of handwritten notes about Soviet military aircraft designs. Tolkachev wrote his full name and address. He risked telling his full identity because he wanted to show he was truly interested in helping the CIA. This letter convinced the CIA that Tolkachev was not a Soviet spy. They reached out and began a key partnership that lasted for seven years.

FISHING FOR SECRETS

Dmitri Polyakov was a Soviet military intelligence officer. He was also a spy for the United States. He worked in Moscow and New York. He was a top official, so he saw lots of classified papers. Sometimes he went on fishing trips with CIA agents to record what he learned. He would sit by the water and talk while an agent held a fishing pole. A device hidden in the top of the pole recorded what Polyakov said. Then the recordings would go to the CIA. Polyakov found out so much information that it filled 25 file drawers at the CIA office. He found out many Soviet secrets about missiles, armed forces, and undercover spies in the United States.

▲ **The Soviet Union would sometimes have military parades to show off some of its weapons.**

Tolkachev was an aircraft expert for the Soviets. At work, he saw graphs and formulas about Soviet designs. He copied the details and test results from their experiments to give to the CIA. He often stuffed papers from work into his coat and took them home. Then, he took photos of them with a special CIA camera. Sometimes he made handwritten notes and copies of graphs.

Then he would deliver the information to the CIA at a certain time and place. His first in-person meeting with a CIA agent was on New Year's Day in 1979. He had a stack of 91 papers shoved under his coat that he handed over.

Over time, Tolkachev delivered hundreds of rolls of film and hundreds of handwritten notes to the CIA. His information was very valuable to the U.S. military. From Tolkachev, the United States learned how some of its missiles and planes could fly nearby without the Soviets knowing. It also learned about advanced Soviet weapon systems.

THINK ABOUT IT

► How is the Cold War different from other wars? How might the differences change the way spies worked?
► Do you think the United States and Soviet Union were right to spy on each other during the Cold War? Explain your answer.
► Is it possible the Cold War might have been different if there were no spies? Explain your answer.

GLOSSARY

classified (KLASS-uh-fide): Classified information is often kept secret to protect people. Spies searched for classified information about other countries and governments.

communism (KAHM-yoo-niz-uhm): Communism is a political system where the government controls many things. The Soviet Union believed in communism.

embassy (EM-buh-see): An embassy is a building in one country with offices for leaders of another country. The agent worked for the U.S. embassy in Moscow.

engineer (en-juh-NEER): An engineer is a person who designs, creates, or builds machines. Tolkachev was an engineer.

intelligence (in-TEL-ih-jenss): Intelligence is information related to an enemy. The spy gathered intelligence.

missile (MIS-uhl): A missile is a type of weapon that aims at long-distance targets. The Soviets wanted to build missile launch sites.

negotiate (ni-GOH-shee-ayt): To negotiate means to solve a disagreement by talking. Kennedy hoped to negotiate with the Soviet Union to avoid a real war.

nuclear (NOO-klee-ur): Nuclear has do to with energy that is created when atoms are split. Nuclear weapons are extremely powerful.

Soviet Union (SOH-vee-et YOON-yuhn): The Soviet Union was a country that had many republics, including Russia. The United States and the Soviet Union were in a Cold War.

TO LEARN MORE

BOOKS

Bearce, Stephanie. *The Cold War*. Waco, TX: Prufrock Press, 2015.

Hyde, Natalie. *The Cold War and the Cuban Missile Crisis*.
New York, NY: Crabtree Publishing, 2016.

Otfinoski, Steven. *The Cold War*. New York, NY: Scholastic, 2018.

WEBSITES

Visit our website for links about the Cold War: childsworld.com/links

Note to Parents, Teachers, and Librarians: We routinely verify our Web links to make sure they are safe and active sites. So encourage your readers to check them out!

SELECTED BIBLIOGRAPHY

Mundy, Liza. "The Women Code Breakers Who Unmasked Soviet Spies." *Smithsonian*, Sept. 2018, smithsonianmag.com. Accessed 15 Nov. 2019.

Royden, Barry G. "Tolkachev, a Worthy Successor to Penkovsky." *Central Intelligence Agency*, 27 June 2008, cia.gov. Accessed 15 Nov. 2019.

"Trigon: Spies Passing in the Night." *Central Intelligence Agency*, 20 June 2016, cia.gov. Accessed 25 Nov. 2019.

INDEX

ABOUT THE AUTHOR

Emma Huddleston lives in Minnesota with her husband. She enjoys writing children's books, and she thinks spies are a fascinating part of history!